T0198908

Venus the Global Child
Family Nicknames

Written by:
Ailin Iwan

Illustrated by:
Cecilia Paplinskie

AuthorHouse™
1663 Liberty Drive
Bloomington, IN 47403
www.authorhouse.com
Phone: 833-262-8899

Because of the dynamic nature of the Internet, any web addresses or links contained in this book may have changed since publication and may no longer be valid. The views expressed in this work are solely those of the author and do not necessarily reflect the views of the publisher, and the publisher hereby disclaims any responsibility for them.

This book is printed on acid-free paper.

ISBN: 978-1-4490-4675-0 (sc)

Print information available on the last page.

Published by AuthorHouse   06/15/2023

authorHOUSE®

This book is dedicated to all children around the world.
You are God's precious creations and our hope for the future.

Global Citizenship Perspective

In the 21st Century, our world is connected through technological advancements. All of the new innovations such as Google, Skype, Facebook, and many others allow us to exchange ideas, information, and cultures at a fast rate across the world. Advancements in the transportation technology have resulted in an increasing number of people moving from one country to another easily. The positive effect is more individuals start to understand, appreciate, and embrace each other's cultures, while they gain more insight about other people's origins, relative to their own. Thus, it is important for people, especially children, to broaden their view of citizenship beyond their country of origin and cultural heritage.

People are starting to realize that they can no longer identify themselves as being from one particular culture or nation. There are multileveled and multilayered identities in each individual. Many people live in transnational spaces which blur the rigid distinction of culture and citizenship.

I hope that while you are reading *Venus, the Global Child*, with your children, you will find the opportunity to talk with them about your own cultural heritage. I also hope that you will encourage your children to have a global perspective and greater appreciation of other cultures.

All the best,

Ailin Iwan

My name is Venus Indah van Bastian.
My Chinese name is Chang Ai Mei.
I am four and a half years old.

My dad is European African and his name is Chuck van Bastian. Everybody calls him Chuck, except my mom, who calls him Sweetheart. I call him Papi

My mom is Chinese Indonesian,
her name is Nirmala Chang.
Her Chinese name is Chang Bai Ai.
Her friends call her Nirmala,
her parents call her Bai Ai,
Papi calls her Honey,
and I call her Mami.

Mami ~ Mother   Papi ~ Father

I call my mother's mom Ama. Ama is a nickname for grandmother in Chinese. Ama's real name is Wulandari Cahyani. My Ama is a native Indonesian and she likes to wear Kebaya, which makes her look so pretty.

Ama ~ Popo ~ Ngen-ngen ~ Grandmother

I call my mother's father Engkong. Engkong is a nickname for grandfather in Chinese. Engkong's real name is Chang Jun Ru. My Engkong originally comes from China. He came to Indonesia with his dad when he was only 13 years old. He is a merchant and owns a store that sells toys. He often sends me new toys for Christmas and Chinese New Year.

Engkong ~ Kung-Kung ~ Yeye ~ Grandfather

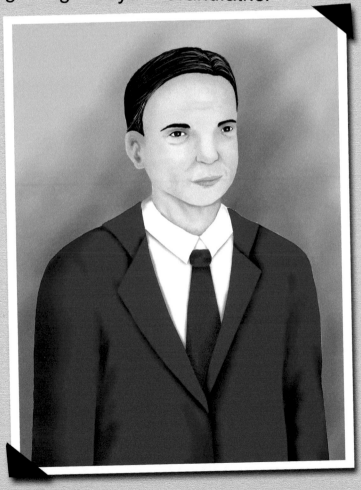

I call my father's mom Oma. Oma is a nickname for grandmother in Dutch. Oma's real name is Chika Adannaya. My Oma is from Nigeria. Her skin is dark, her hair is curly, and her face is so sweet and kind. Oma is very fashionable and she loves to send me lots of new clothes of her own design.

Oma ~ Grandmother ~ Granny

I call my father's dad Opa. Opa is a nickname of grandfather in Dutch. My Opa was born in America but all his relatives live in the Netherlands. Opa's real name is Albert van Bastian. He likes sport and his favorite game is football.
My Opa is truly funny and he likes to tell jokes.

Opa ~ Grandfather ~ Grandpa

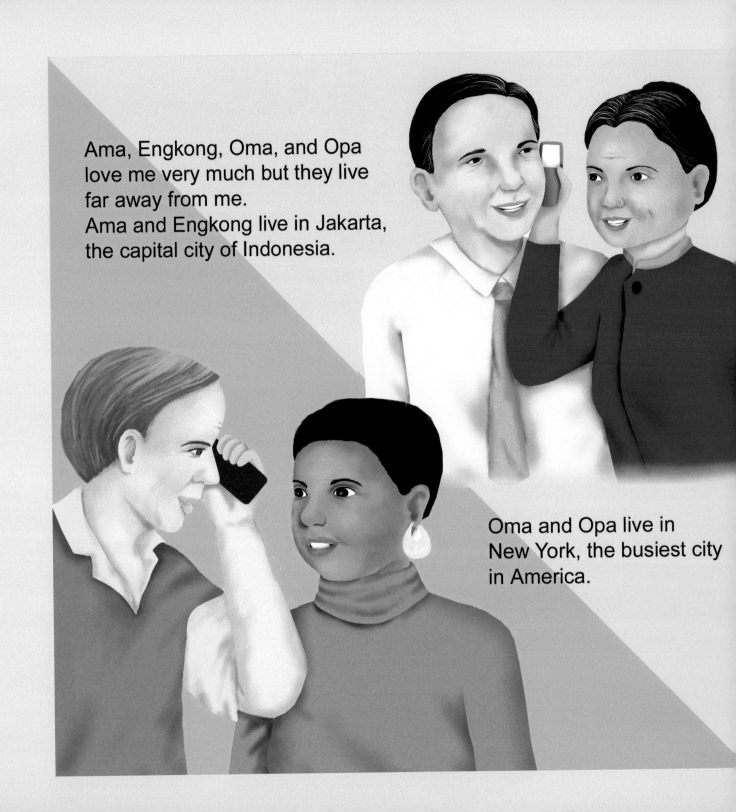

Ama, Engkong, Oma, and Opa love me very much but they live far away from me.
Ama and Engkong live in Jakarta, the capital city of Indonesia.

Oma and Opa live in New York, the busiest city in America.

I often talk to them on the phone and
I visit them during my vacations.
Papi, Mami and I live in San Francisco.

I also have nicknames. My friends call me Venus.
Sometimes my Mami and Papi call me Ai Mei
but often times they call me Sweetie.
Ama and Engkong always call me Xiao Mei
(Xiao Mei means little sister or little girl).
Oma and Opa call me Cutie Pie.

Mami and Papi tell me that
Venus Indah means the same
as Ai Mei. My name means
beautiful love because
Mami and Papi think that I am a
gift from God for their beautiful love.

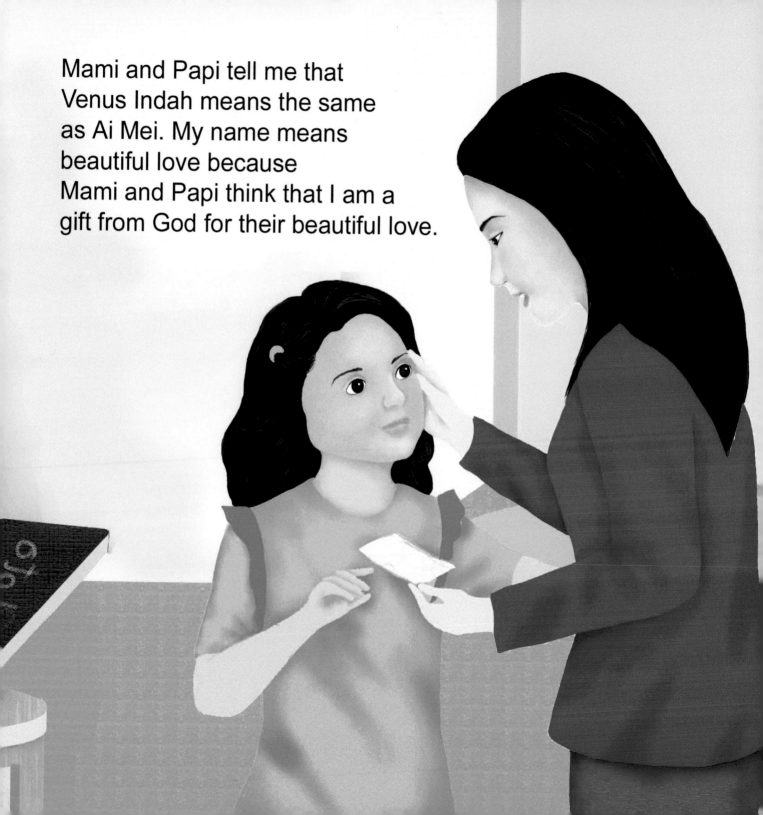

Printed in the United States
by Baker & Taylor Publisher Services